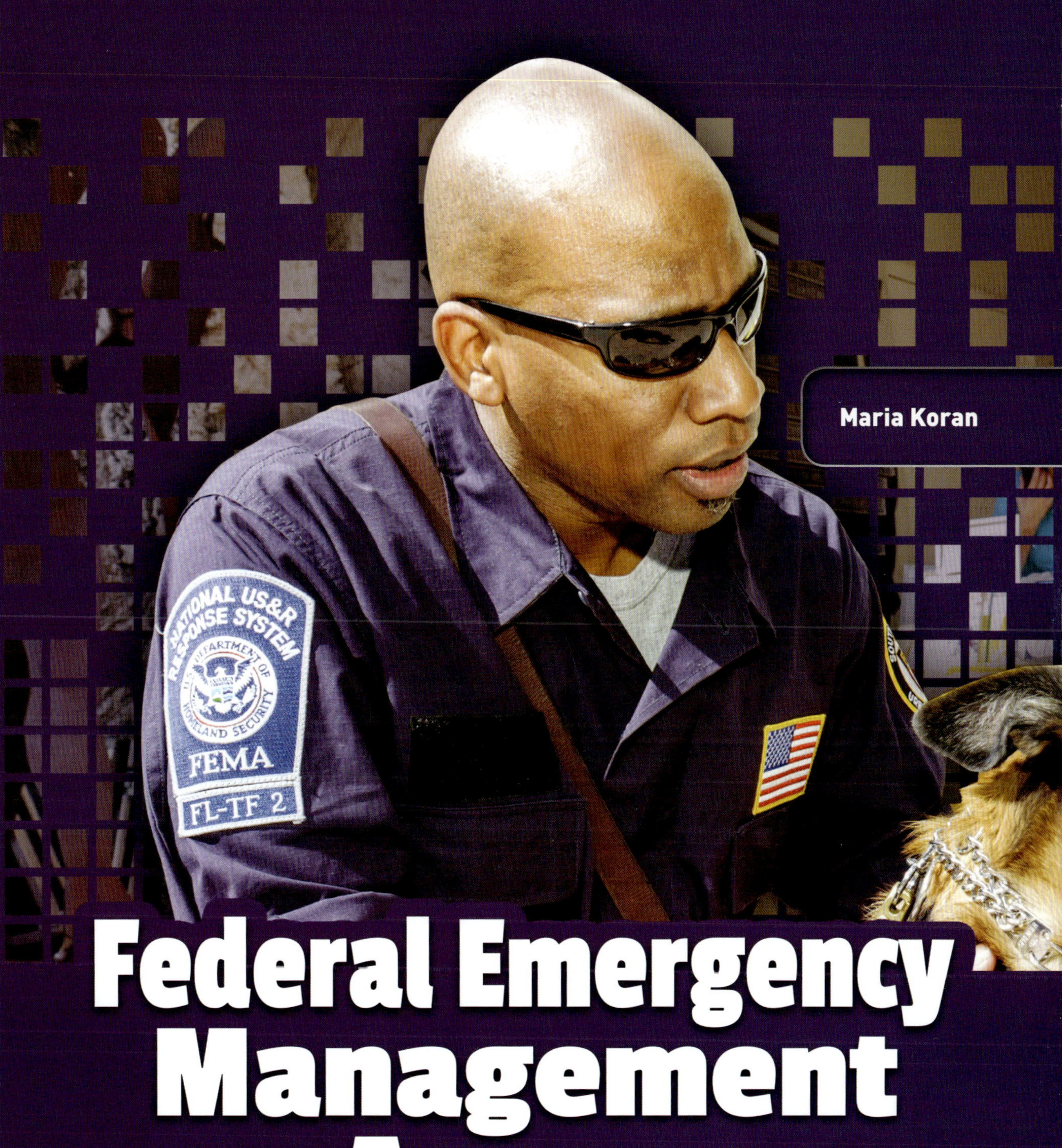

Maria Koran

Federal Emergency Management Agency

POWER • AUTHORITY • GOVERNANCE

LIGHTBOX
openlightbox.com

Go to **www.openlightbox.com** and enter this book's unique code.

ACCESS CODE

LBXW5725

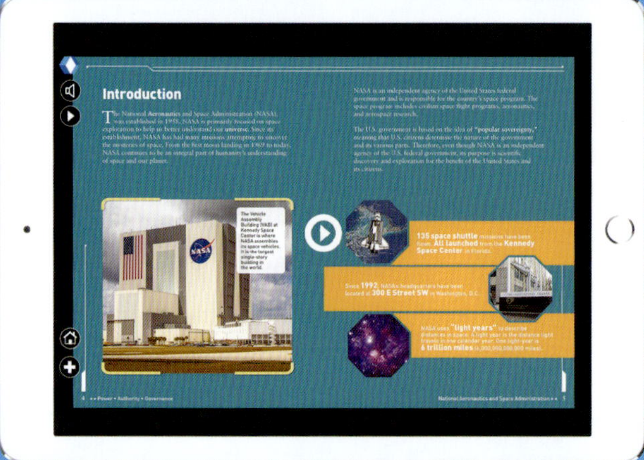

Lightbox is an all-inclusive digital solution for the teaching and learning of curriculum topics in an original, groundbreaking way. Lightbox is based on National Curriculum Standards.

STANDARD FEATURES OF LIGHTBOX

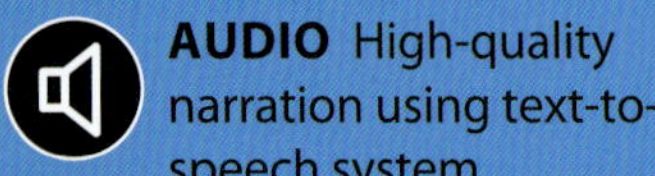
AUDIO High-quality narration using text-to-speech system

WEBLINKS Curated links to external, child-safe resources

INTERACTIVE MAPS Interactive maps and aerial satellite imagery

VIDEOS Embedded high-definition video clips

SLIDESHOWS Pictorial overviews of key concepts

QUIZZES Ten multiple choice questions that are automatically graded and emailed for teacher assessment

ACTIVITIES Printable PDFs that can be emailed and graded

TRANSPARENCIES Step-by-step layering of maps, diagrams, charts, and timelines

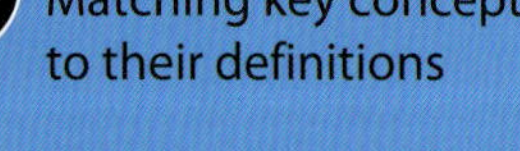
KEY WORDS Matching key concepts to their definitions

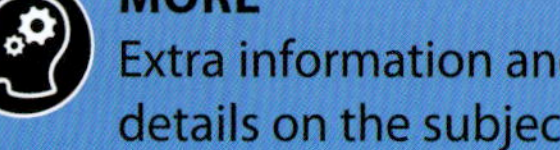
MORE Extra information and details on the subject

FIRST HAND Letters, diaries, and other primary sources

DOCS Speeches, newspaper articles, and other historical documents

POWER • AUTHORITY • GOVERNANCE

Federal Emergency Management Agency

CONTENTS

Introduction

Natural disasters have always been with us. But in the United States, there was no government department whose job it was to help. That changed on April 1, 1979. Today, we have the Federal Emergency Management Agency (FEMA).

FEMA is the federal agency that helps people after a natural disaster. They are not a law enforcement agency and cannot arrest anyone. FEMA's mission is, "Helping people before, during, and after disasters." In recent years, they have been very busy.

FEMA's goal is to keep people safe. Since natural disasters are so complicated, FEMA works with other agencies, too. Agencies such as the Environmental Protection Agency (EPA) check for **contamination**. The Food and Drug Administration (FDA) checks the food supply. Working together, FEMA can help more people. FEMA is also a part of the Department of Homeland Security (DHS).

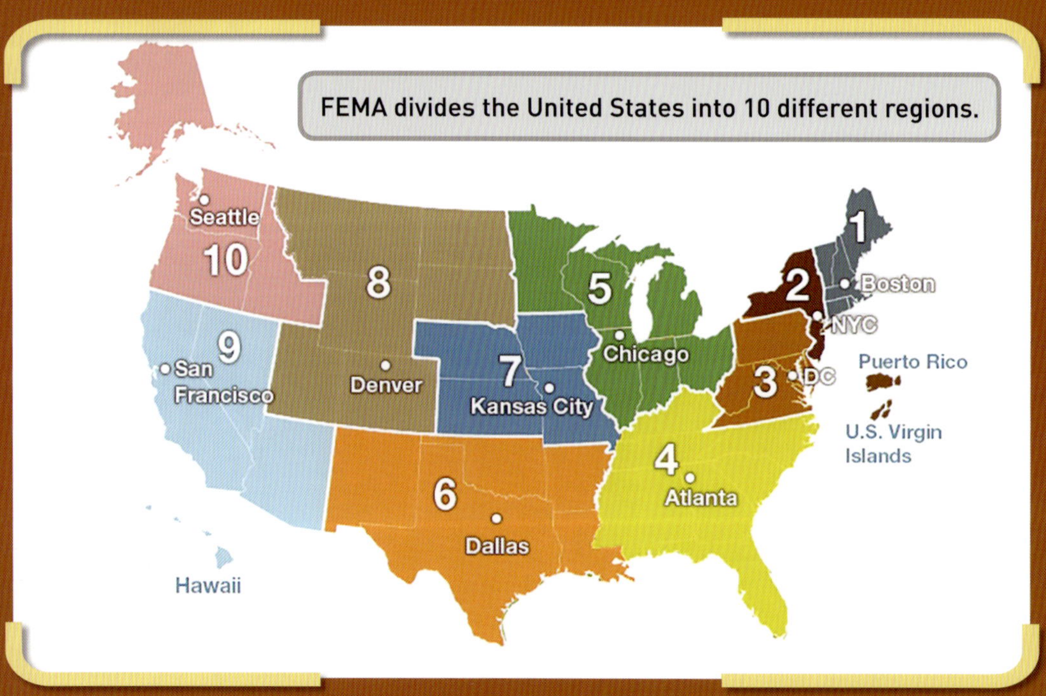

Although the **executive branch** of government has the ability to create departments such as FEMA when needed, the authority to do so actually comes from the people of the United States. The idea that the authority of a government is given to it by its people is called **"popular sovereignty."** This also means that government leaders and organizations must always obey the U.S. **Constitution**.

FEMA must be careful when responding to a disaster. The agency is working with people when they are at their most vulnerable. FEMA must respect a person's right to privacy while trying to help. This right is guaranteed by the **Fourth Amendment** to the Constitution.

FEMA is one of **22** agencies that work together under the **Department of Homeland Security (DHS)**.

DHS is a huge department. Its headquarters is the **largest** construction project in Washington, D.C. since the **Pentagon** was built.

The U.S. Constitution is a short document. The original document only has **four pages**. Its best-known part is **the Preamble**.

Origins of FEMA

The origins of FEMA go back more than 200 years. In 1803, a congressional act was passed to help a town in New Hampshire after a terrible fire. That was the first piece of disaster relief legislation in the United States. Over the next century, **Congress** passed more than 100 bills to help after disasters. However, they did not create an agency to manage these disasters when they happen.

President Carter was captain of a nuclear submarine while he was in the U.S. Navy.

Many years later, Congress passed a wide-reaching bill with the Federal Disaster Relief Program of 1950. Although this bill helped, it was still not enough. Congress then passed the Disaster Relief Act of 1966. Sadly, the 1960s and 1970s had massive natural disasters. Something had to be done. President Jimmy Carter created FEMA on March 31, 1979. On July 15, 1979, he transferred all disaster authority to FEMA.

The **terrorist** attacks of September 11, 2001 brought more changes to FEMA. In March 2003, FEMA joined 22 other federal agencies to become the new Department of Homeland Security. FEMA's job was to make sure that first responders were trained and well-equipped. This training is not just for natural disasters. FEMA also makes sure they can deal with weapons used by terrorists. FEMA must plan for any kind of disaster.

On October 4, 2006, President George W. Bush signed the Post-Katrina Emergency Reform Act. This was after the devastation of Hurricane Katrina. This Act reorganized FEMA again by giving it new authority and power.

Branches of Government

The Department of Homeland Security is a **cabinet** post in the executive branch of government. This means that FEMA reports to the secretary of homeland security. In 2019, the acting secretary of the department was Kevin McAleenan. Since DHS is part of the executive branch, Mr. McAleenan reports to the president.

The U.S. government is organized so that no one of the three branches has unlimited power. This system is known as "**checks and balances**." The idea is that each branch can "check" the power of the other two. This gives "balance" to the government.

Congress controls the budget of DHS, and DHS controls FEMA. Additionally, Congress has the power to investigate both.

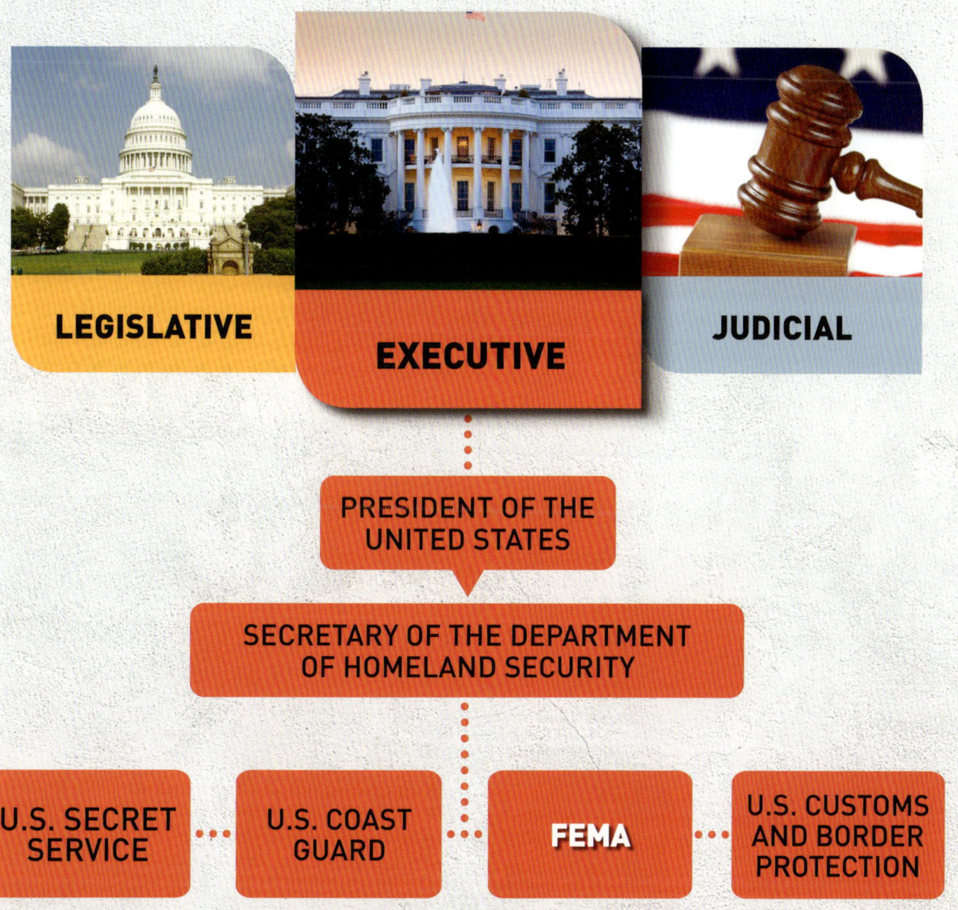

Purpose of FEMA

FEMA's mission is to help U.S. citizens before, during, and after disasters. Since it became a member of DHS in 2003, it also trains and supports the country's first responders. FEMA prepares for any kind of disaster, natural or man-made.

FEMA's emergency resources and support are widespread. They include transportation, communication, supplies, public safety, and security. To provide these resources, FEMA divides its mission into three parts, Prevent, Respond, and Recover. Hurricanes are a good example of how FEMA implements this response plan.

First, FEMA wants to prevent damage. To do this, they give information about preparing for a hurricane. This preparation includes information including what to put in your hurricane kit, what the evacuation routes are, and how to get a hurricane alert. FEMA gives constant updates on its website. Second, FEMA responds to the hurricane. They work with local authorities to help with evacuations, security, emergency supplies, and temporary housing. Finally, FEMA helps in the recovery after the hurricane. The agency helps with the clean up and even gives loans to families.

Hurricanes are rated in five categories. One is the weakest and five the strongest.

It is FEMA's job to help people. But where does it get the authority and power to do this? FEMA gets its authority from the Preamble to the Constitution.

Hurricane Irma

In September 2017, the **Gulf Coast** was hit by Hurricane Irma. This was one of the most devastating natural disasters in U.S. history. FEMA helped after the storm in several ways. FEMA's Individuals and Households Program provided about $1 billion for Florida alone. This does not include money for other states that were also badly damaged.

FEMA Through the Years

Since it began in 1979, FEMA has responded to thousands of disasters. Some have been natural events. Others, such are crashes or spills, are man-made.

March 28, 1979

The Three Mile Island nuclear power plant has a partial meltdown. Radiation is released. FEMA helps with the recovery.

March 31, 1979

President Jimmy Carter creates FEMA by executive order in response to massive natural disasters.

1988

Yellowstone National Park has wildfires that cover 793,880 acres of the park. FEMA helps with recovery.

August 1992

FEMA responds to the enormous Category 5 Hurricane Andrew when it hits Louisiana, Florida, and the Bahamas.

April 19, 1995

A bomb explodes in Oklahoma City, causing one of the largest man-made disasters in U.S. history.

February 26, 1996

FEMA is elevated to a cabinet position.

November 12, 2001

American Airlines flight 587 crashes while flying from New York City to Los Angeles. All 260 on board were killed. FEMA provides disaster relief services to their families.

March 1, 2003

FEMA becomes part of the Department of Homeland Security.

August 29, 2005

Hurricane Katrina hits the coast of Louisiana near New Orleans. It remains one of the most destructive disasters in U.S. history. FEMA helps the millions of people that were affected by the hurricane.

December 2007

The Great Recession begins, leading to more than 8 million Americans losing their jobs. It also makes disaster relief more difficult for many communities.

January 2015

The North American Blizzard comes ashore in the Pacific Northwest, moves across the United States, and joins a No'r Easter storm in New England. FEMA is called in to help people across the country.

October 2017

The "California Firestorm" rages uncontrolled for days and burns more than a quarter of a million acres. 44 people die. FEMA helps with the recovery.

October 2018

Hurricane Michael causes enormous amounts of destruction throughout the United States and Central America. FEMA provides both national and international aid.

FEMA Issues

FEMA's mission is to help people before, during, and after a disaster. They are often heroes to the people they help. However, no organization is perfect. FEMA has faced issues during its history.

After Superstorm Sandy in 2012, there were complaints against FEMA. It was said they were not managing costs well and were inefficient. Costs were $150 million more than expected and repairs were two years overdue. However, this was not all FEMA's fault. The city of New York had to repay FEMA $5.3 million dollars for making false claims. The city asked FEMA for money to replace vehicles destroyed during the storm. However, none of those vehicles were working before the storm hit. Many felt that New York City had cheated FEMA.

FEMA has also made mistakes. In October 2018, Hurricane Michael went ashore on the Florida Panhandle. Entire communities were destroyed. At least 35 people were killed. Damage was estimated around $10.4 billion. However, FEMA gave only $1.8 million dollars to the city of Panama City to rebuild.

FEMA has been accused of not distributing resources fairly to racial minorities such as African Americans and Latinos.

FEMA is often accused of not distributing resources and money fairly. It has worked very hard to make sure that the agency now distributes aid fairly to all regions and citizens of the United States.

Checks and the Preamble

When we study a federal agency, it can seem like they have unlimited power. However, when FEMA comes to a disaster site, it does not take over. The government's system of "checks and balances" applies to agencies, too.

FEMA applies its authority from the Preamble to the Constitution in several ways.

- Maintain order and security, keep property and people safe
  Preamble topic: domestic tranquility, common defense
- Stop price gouging for supplies
  Preamble topic: establish justice
- Provide food and shelter
  Preamble topic: general welfare
- Provide financial assistance
  Preamble topic: general welfare

People affected by disasters are normally very happy to receive FEMA's help. However, if a FEMA official should act inappropriately, what could you as a **civilian** do? The answer is that you can simply ask them to stop or refuse their assistance. FEMA has no power like local police do. They only want to help the community recover. There are plenty of checks in place. FEMA answers to DHS. DHS answers to the president. Congress can investigate both DHS and FEMA.

Key Figures in FEMA

Many notable people have made important contributions to the safety of the United States while working for FEMA. Many have been FEMA administrators.

Gordon Vickery

Gordon Vickery (1920–1996) President Jimmy Carter appointed him the first administrator of FEMA, a position he only held as acting administrator from April 1979 until July 1979. Vickery was better known as the fire chief of Seattle, Washington, a post he held for 34 years before going to Washington, D.C.

Julius Becton Jr.

Julius W. Becton, Jr. (1926–) FEMA was still a very young agency when President Reagan made him administrator of FEMA in 1985. It was dealing with confusion from several agencies being combined. Becton was a three-star general. He had retired from the U.S. Army after nearly 40 years. Becton brought order to the organization.

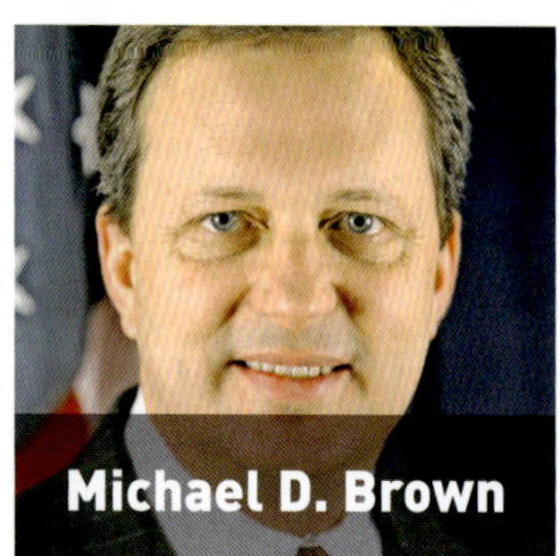

Michael D. Brown

Michael D. Brown (1954–) President George W. Bush placed him as the administrator of FEMA on April 15, 2003 just as it was joining the DHS. His tenure at FEMA was rocky. He resigned within days after Hurricane Katrina.

Brown v Katrina

HISTORICAL CASE STUDY

Michael D. Brown's time as the administrator was very uneasy. Unlike previous administrators, Brown had no experience in emergency management. He was a lawyer. However, when President Bush nominated him for the position, Brown was not practicing law. He had been the commissioner of the International Arabian Horse Association.

While administrator of FEMA, Brown was harshly criticized for the way he handled 2004's Hurricane Frances. He mishandled disaster relief funds after the hurricane. FEMA overpaid on many claims when the real damage was only slight. People suggested that the repair companies were Brown's business associates. However, it was Hurricane Katrina that ended his time as administrator.

Hurricane Katrina hit New Orleans on August 29, 2005. It was a historic disaster. The Bush administration was condemned for its lack of response. However, this was not all Mr. Brown's fault. FEMA had just joined DHS. There was confusion about who should be in charge. Brown was not put in charge of relief efforts until August 31st. The delay greatly slowed relief efforts.

Even after he arrived, there was no active response from FEMA. Civilians were trying to save each other while the nation watched on television. Brown was replaced in New Orleans on September 7th and recalled to Washington, D.C. on the 9th. He resigned as administrator of FEMA on September 12, 2005. Many people had died during the disaster. Trust in the federal government was at an all-time low among the people of the Gulf Coast.

More than 1,200 people died due to Hurricane Katrina.

Careers in FEMA

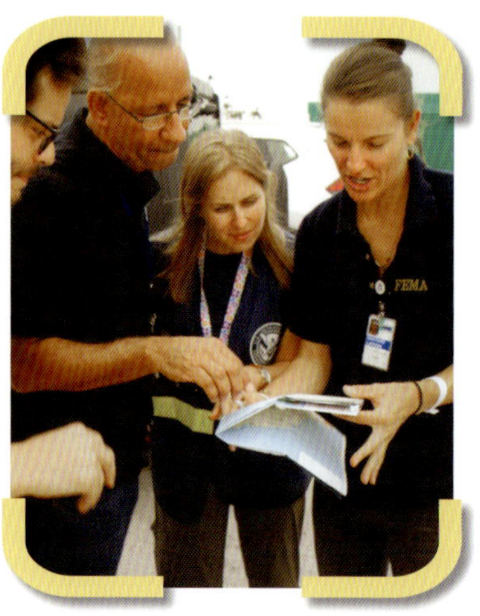

Emergency Management Specialist

FEMA Emergency Management Specialists (EMSs) can play many roles. They may work to help people get ready when a disaster is coming. During an emergency, they might manage rescue workers. They might get supplies to people who need them. After a disaster, they help make things safe and help communities recover.

Environmental Protection Specialist

Natural disasters have a huge impact on our land, water, and air. That impact can be dangerous to humans and animals. Environmental Protection Specialists (EPSs) study those impacts so the agency can help make things safe after a disaster.

Reservist

When a disaster strikes, FEMA needs extra workers fast. Construction workers, social workers, lawyers, truck drivers, and many others are needed. FEMA relies on these "reservists." They are hired to work after a disaster. They are temporary workers who stay as long as they are needed.

Carpenter

FEMA often sends skilled workers, including carpenters, to emergency sites. They set up command centers, build shelters, and help rebuild damaged areas. The carpenters hired by FEMA are often from the community affected by the disaster.

In **2018**, FEMA's budget was **$18.4 billion**. That money was distributed according to where disasters happened.

Each administrator of FEMA is appointed by the president and then confirmed by the United States Senate. They have **no term limits**.

STEM stands for Science, Technology, Engineering, and Math. Of the hundreds of careers at FEMA, **all of them** depend on STEM.

Tools of the Trade

FEMA requires many different types of tools and devices to do its job. Some of these tools are medical. Others include earth-moving equipment. Still others include common farm equipment, or even baby bottles for feeding young animals.

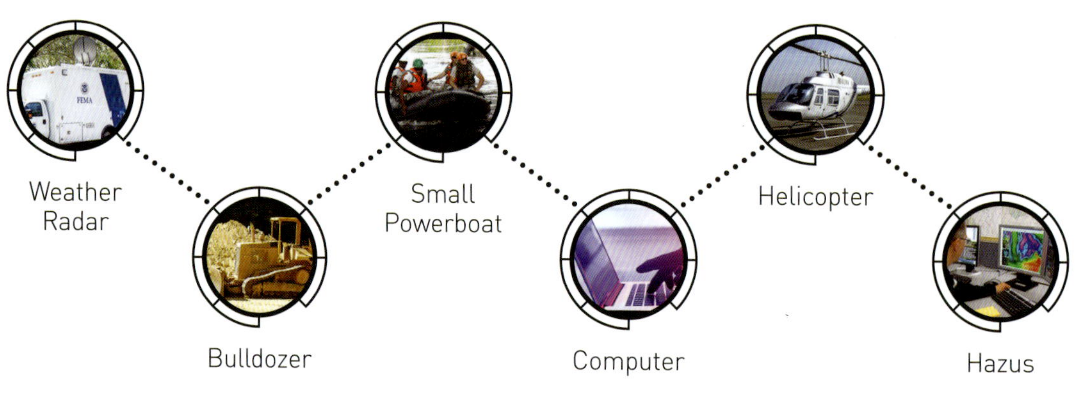

Weather Radar

Weather forecasters use weather radar to track storms. The radar shows where a storm is and where it is likely to go. It also helps show how large a storm is. This helps FEMA figure out who will be affected and how best to help them.

Bulldozer

Bulldozers can move a lot of material at once. They can be helpful before and after natural disasters. Bulldozers can be used to move earth and rocks to strengthen **levees** and prevent flooding. They can also be used to clear debris after a disaster.

Small Powerboat

Small powerboats are useful during floods. They can go places big boats or vehicles cannot. Boats can be used to rescue people or animals stranded by the flood. They can also be used to carry supplies or rescue workers into flooded areas.

Computer

FEMA gathers lots of data. It uses computers to store and go through the data. Computers help FEMA make sense of the data it collects. FEMA looks for any issues that the data may show. The agency can then improve how it handles emergencies.

Helicopter

Sometimes, a helicopter is the only way to get people or supplies in or out of an emergency site. Helicopters can carry heavy loads of supplies into remote areas. Since they can hover, they can be used to rescue people trapped by water or uneven ground.

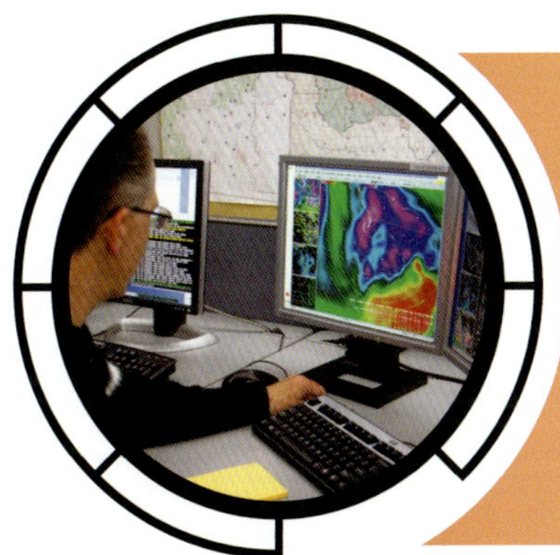

Hazus

Hazus is a **software program** developed by FEMA. It can predict the effects of earthquakes, floods, and hurricanes. FEMA offers Hazus as a free download to anyone. Local authorities can use it to help their communities.

FEMA in the United States

FEMA works across the United States. This means they must work and cooperate with many different agencies and organizations. FEMA works with both health organizations and local law enforcement.

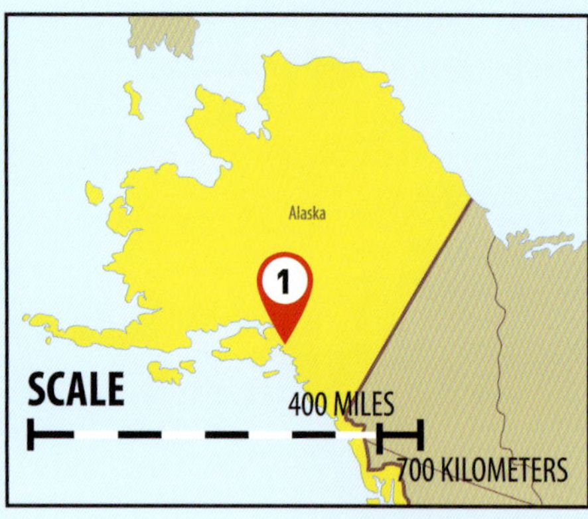

1 Prince William Sound, Alaska

On March 24, 1989, the oil tanker *Exxon Valdez* struck a reef in Prince William Sound, Alaska. Eleven million gallons of crude oil spilled into the clear water. It was the worst oil spill in U.S. history at the time. FEMA worked with the EPA and many other services to try to contain and clean the disaster site. However, hundreds of thousands of marine birds and animals were killed.

2 Los Angeles, California

In November 2018, California suffered its worst wildfire. Hundreds of thousands of acres were burned. Entire towns were destroyed. More than 80 people died. FEMA worked with dozens of other agencies during the weeks that the fires raged.

Love Canal, New York

Love Canal, New York was the location of a major ecological disaster that required the help of FEMA. In 1978, thousands of gallons of **toxic** waste were released into the community. FEMA provided millions of dollars of assistance for housing, food, water, and health assistance. To provide the needed assistance, FEMA worked with many other agencies such as the EPA and the FDA.

Florida

On August 24, 1992, Hurricane Andrew hit southern Florida as a Category 5 hurricane. 44 people lost their lives. Entire towns were washed away. Damages from the hurricane were estimated to be over $25 billion dollars. Even with FEMA's help, it took many years for this part of the country to recover.

FEMA in the World

FEMA is responsible for handling natural disasters in the United States and its territories. Sometimes the United States needs help when disaster strikes. Other countries are quick to offer money and supplies. Part of FEMA's job is now working with other countries to manage those donations. Foreign countries sent hundreds of millions of dollars to help the United States after Hurricane Katrina hit in 2005. They also sent thousands of pounds of supplies.

On August 5, 2017, Hurricane Harvey landed in Texas. It was a Category 4 storm that did millions of dollars in damage. The government of Canada offered to help. FEMA worked with them to get the 27,000 pounds of supplies they donated to hurricane victims.

The Canadian government sent many different kinds of supplies, including baby formula, to the United States after Hurricane Harvey.

Between August and October 2017, the United States was hit by five hurricanes. Those were named Harvey, Irma, Jose, Maria, and Nate. Hurricanes also hit Mexico, but they still offered to send aid. They sent drinking water and bug spray to help U.S. storm victims.

FEMA also helps many other countries when they have disasters of their own. The United States donates millions of dollars each year to help disasters all around the world. FEMA also shares its Hazus computer system with other countries, including Canada and Mexico, to help them prepare for and respond to national disasters.

FEMA's headquarters are located at **500 C St. S.W.** in Washington, D.C.

Cyclone Idai hit southeast Africa in March 2019. It is considered by many to be the **largest natural disaster** in the southern hemisphere. The citizens of Africa used FEMA's Hazus computer system to organize their recovery.

FEMA helped the citizens of Indonesia after a devastating **earthquake** and **tsunami** in **2018**.

FEMA Today

FEMA works to keep up with a changing world. New technology offers advances in predicting the weather and possible earthquakes. This helps FEMA prepare for disasters. However, the biggest change for FEMA has been their role as a member of DHS.

Ever since the attacks on September 11, 2001, the United States has had a different outlook on the world. Before, many Americans felt protected by two oceans. Losing the Twin Towers in New York City shattered that feeling of safety. DHS's priority is to prepare for terrorist attacks. FEMA's mission is "Helping people before, during, and after disasters," so their role in DHS is easy to understand.

The last several years have challenged FEMA. Hurricanes, wildfires, floods, mudslides, and blizzards have been at record numbers. FEMA's resources are greatly in demand. The agency has a serious need for funding in order to do its job well. Because FEMA is no longer independent, it has to share the DHS budget with 21 other agencies.

How FEMA will meet these challenges is the question for today's agency. The United States depends on FEMA today. In the future, the nation may need the agency even more.

FEMA spent $87 million to assist with debris removal from the World Trade Center site after the September 11th attack.

Puerto Rico and Hurricanes Irma and Maria

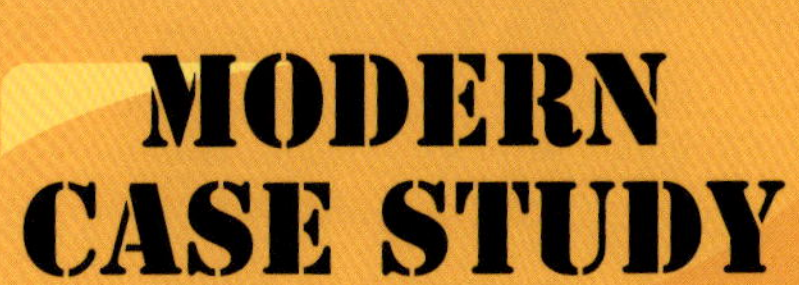

On September 6, 2017, Category 5 Hurricane Irma rolled over the U.S. Virgin Islands and then the U.S. territory of Puerto Rico. Exactly two weeks later, before the people had a chance to recover, Category 4 Hurricane Maria hit. The islands were devastated. However, the U.S. mainland had also been dealt a deadly blow.

As U.S. citizens, the people on the islands deserved the same protection and assistance from the government as citizens on the mainland. However, since Puerto Rico is not a state, what types of assistance should FEMA be able to provide? That was a decision for the president and FEMA to make.

Because of Puerto Rico's status as a territory of the United States, there was great confusion about the disaster aid that was sent to the island. The result was that, almost a year later, many people on Puerto Rico still did not have water or electricity. The response to the hurricanes in Puerto Rico has resulted in FEMA reassessing how aid is provided to the territories of the United States, and not just the country's states.

Puerto Rico is one of several U.S. territories in the Caribbean.

U.S. citizens in Puerto Rico were left stranded for months.

FEMA Looking to the Future

FEMA tries to live up to its mission statement. Today's FEMA is preparing for tomorrow's emergencies. It faces serious challenges. Each year there are natural and man-made disasters in many different parts of the United States.

FEMA's National Flood Insurance Program helps people when their homes are damaged.

FEMA uses technology and data to predict the effects of natural disasters. New predictions reveal new threats. For example, deep floods may be predicted around a town that has not been flooded before. The people in that town will not know what to do. It is FEMA's job to help them try to keep the floodwaters out. If the town floods, it will be FEMA's job to help them recover.

Unfortunately, technology can also be the cause of disasters that FEMA will need to address. As technology and science increase, the potential for man-made disasters also increases. Man-made disasters can come in the form of a new oil pipeline spill or foreign terrorism. FEMA must plan for how advances in technology can result in disasters that will need their help.

As the world becomes more global every day, all countries are expected to help each other with their natural disasters. FEMA's International Affairs Division must expand its mission in the future. It might become, "Helping people all over the world before, during, and after disasters."

FEMA works with volunteer organizations such as the Red Cross to help respond to natural disasters all over the world.

The eruption of a volcano in Guatemala in 2018 was an enormous natural disaster that required help from dozens of countries.

ACTIVITY ★★

Create a Policy Paper

It is almost impossible to predict when a natural disaster will strike. Tornadoes appear without warning. Earthquakes are even more surprising. Some of the deadliest hurricanes develop and hit shore in only a day. What can we do to protect ourselves? If you work for FEMA, this is your daily challenge.

For this activity, pretend that you work for FEMA. You are in charge of preparing your neighborhood for the most likely natural disaster to occur. It certainly is a big job, when you think about it.

Develop your own thoughts about how to prepare your neighborhood, or community, for a natural disaster. No evacuations are possible, so you will need to think of everything. Write a policy paper that outlines your plan. Do not forget about your pets!

Step 1:

Answer the following questions to help you develop your opinion.

1. What is the most likely natural disaster to occur in your community? Why?
2. What are the greatest dangers this type of disaster causes?
3. What kind of supplies would you suggest everybody have in their emergency kit? Why?
4. What preparations could people make that would reduce the damage?
5. Think about dangers that might happen after the disaster passes. What are they?
6. How should your community prepare if they were to be cut off for a week or more?
7. How will you organize your neighbors to work together to recover after the disaster has passed?

Step 2:

Take your ideas from Questions 1 - 7 and write a one-page policy paper. It should explain the policy you think is correct about how your community should prepare for a natural disaster. It should also explain why. Include an introductory paragraph.

- Paragraph 1: What is the question?
- Paragraph 2: What are the issues surrounding the question?
- Paragraph 3: What is your policy on the issue, and why?

QUIZ ★★

1 Which federal department is FEMA a part of?

2 Who was the U.S. president that created FEMA?

3 Which part of the U.S. Constitution gives FEMA its authority?

4 What is FEMA's stated purpose?

5 Name one of the careers available at FEMA.

6 Name two of the agencies that helped FEMA with the Love Canal toxic waste disaster.

7 Which two U.S. Caribbean territories were struck by Hurricane Irma?

8 What are two of FEMA's "Tools of the Trade"?

9 Name the category 4 hurricane that hit Puerto Rico in 2017.

10 Who was the administrator of FEMA when Hurricane Katrina hit New Orleans?

ANSWERS

1. DHS 2. Jimmy Carter 3. The Preamble 4. To help people 5. EMS, EPS, Reservist, Carpenter 6. EPA and FDA 7. Virgin Islands and Puerto Rico 8. Radar, bulldozer, computer, helicopter, Hazus, boat 9. Maria 10. Michael Brown

KEY WORDS ★★

cabinet: a group of people that advise the president of the United States

checks and balances: counterbalancing influences by which a system is regulated.

civilian: a person not in the armed services or the police force

Congress: governing body of the legislative branch of government consisting of two chambers, the House of Representatives and the Senate

Constitution: the supreme law of the United States of America

contamination: to make impure by poisoning or polluting

executive branch: exercises authority and responsibility for the governance of a state. The power of the executive branch falls on the president of the United States.

Fourth Amendment: the amendment to the Constitution that guarantees the right of the people to secure their property against unreasonable searches and seizures

Gulf Coast: the coastline along the southeastern United States and Gulf of Mexico

levees: barriers built to prevent the overflow of a river

popular sovereignty: the idea that the authority of a state and its government are controlled by the people of the state

software program: a set of instructions that allow for a certain type of computer operation

terrorist: a person who uses violence and intimidation, especially against civilians, for political reasons

toxic: poisonous

INDEX ★★

SUPPLEMENTARY RESOURCES

Click on the plus icon ⊕ found in the bottom left corner of each spread to open additional teacher resources.

- Download and print the book's quizzes and activities
- Access curriculum correlations
- Explore additional web applications that enhance the Lightbox experience

LIGHTBOX DIGITAL TITLES

Packed full of integrated media

VIDEOS

INTERACTIVE MAPS

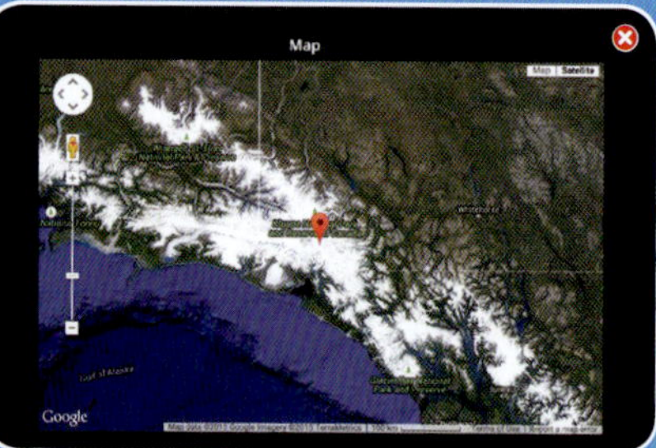

WEBLINKS

SLIDESHOWS

QUIZZES

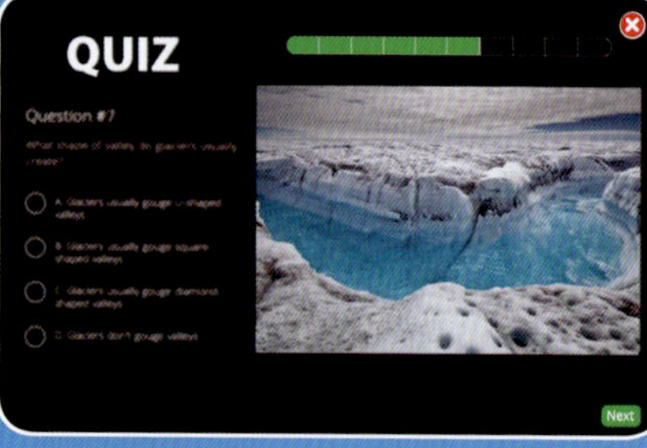

OPTIMIZED FOR

- ✓ TABLETS
- ✓ WHITEBOARDS
- ✓ COMPUTERS
- ✓ AND MUCH MORE!

Published by Smartbook Media Inc.
350 5th Avenue, 59th Floor New York, NY 10118
Website: www.openlightbox.com

Library of Congress Control Number: 2019939795

ISBN 978-1-5105-4686-8 (hardcover)
ISBN 978-1-5105-4687-5 (multi-user eBook)

Printed in Guangzhou, China
1 2 3 4 5 6 7 8 9 0 23 22 21 20 19

052019
122718

Editor: John Willis
Art Director: Terry Paulhus

Every reasonable effort has been made to trace ownership and to obtain permission to reprint copyright material. The publisher would be pleased to have any errors or omissions brought to its attention so that they may be corrected in subsequent printings.

The publisher acknowledges Alamy, Shutterstock, and Wikimedia Commons as its primary image suppliers for this title.